Lingo Dingo
and the
Danish chef

Written by Mark Pallis

Illustrated by James Cottell

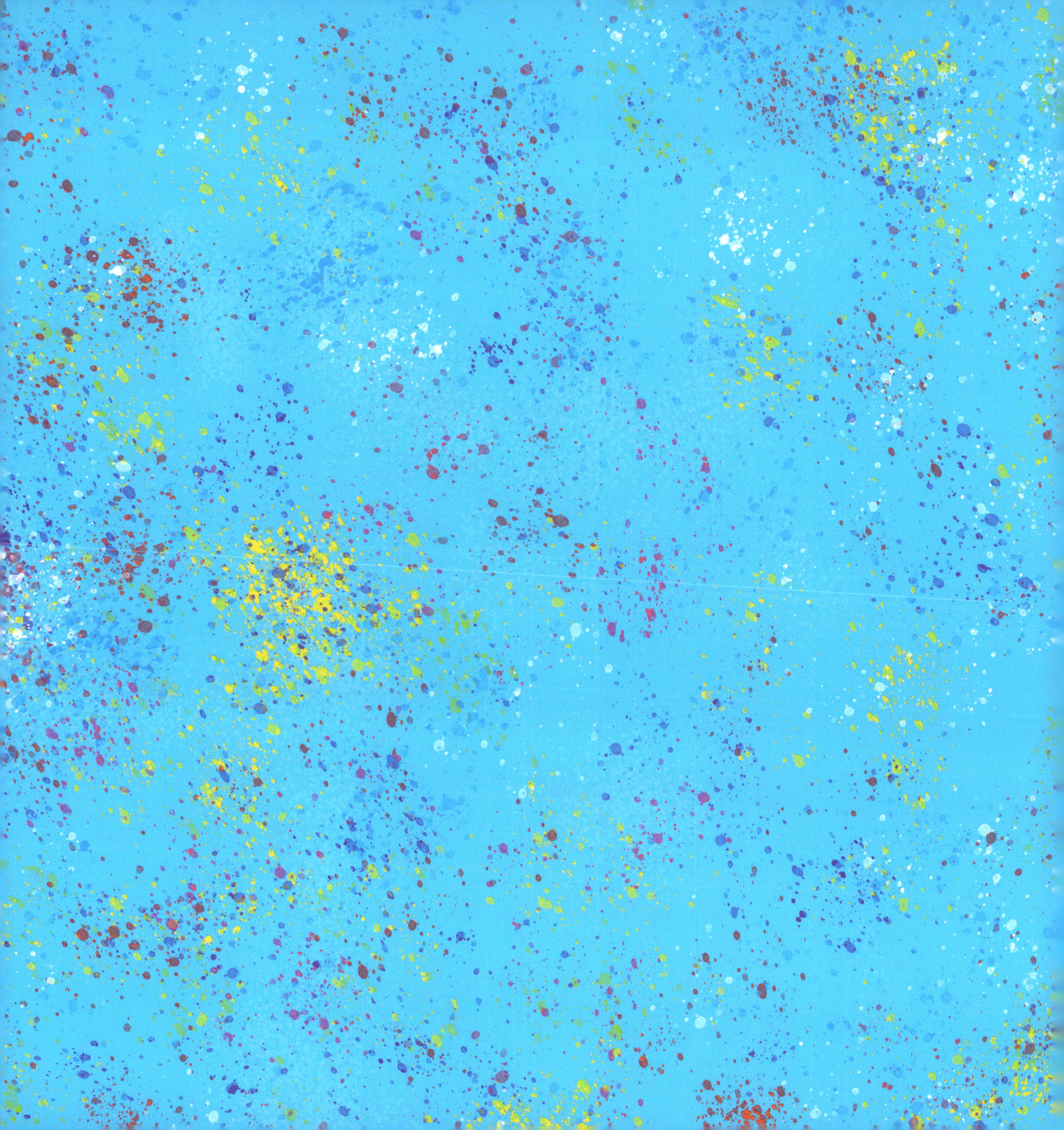

For my awesome sons- MP

For Leo and Juniper - JC

LINGO DINGO AND THE DANISH CHEF

All rights reserved. This book or any portion thereof may not be reproduced or used in any manner whatsoever without the express written permission of the publisher except for the use of brief excerpts in a review.

Story edited by Natascha Biebow, Blue Elephant Storyshaping
First Printing, 2023
ISBN: 978-1-915337-56-6
Neu Westend Press

Lingo Dingo
and the
Danish chef

Written by Mark Pallis
Illustrated by James Cottell

NEU WESTEND PRESS

This is Lingo. She's a Dingo and she loves helping.
Anyone. Anytime. Anyhow.

Lingo often helps her stylish neighbour Gunther, who lives by himself next door. She does a few jobs and has a nice chat. It makes Gunther feel good and it makes Lingo feel good too.

One day, Lingo arranged a special birthday party for Gunther. She even ordered a cake from a famous Danish chef.

There was a knock at the door, "It must be the cake!" said Lingo. But it was a monkey.

"Hej. Mit navn er Chef Peter. Jeg har et problem," he said.

Oh no. I can't speak Danish yet, thought Lingo. *Maybe 'Hej' is like 'Hello'.*

Hej = Hello; **Mit navn er** = My name is
Jeg har et problem = I have a problem

"Hej," said Lingo. Chef Peter replied slowly, "Beklager. Jeg kan ikke lave fødselsdagskagen."

"I don't understand," said Lingo. "But let me guess. You want..."

Beklager = I am sorry; **Jeg kan ikke lave** = I cannot make; **fødselsdagskagen** = the birthday cake

"Min ovn er gået i stykker," explained Chef. "Må jeg bruge din ovn?"

Chef's oven must be broken thought Lingo. "I know! Let's bake the cake together," she said.

Min ovn er gået i stykker = my oven is broken;
Må jeg bruge din ovn? = can I use your oven?

Chef tapped his wrist. "Hvad er klokken? Klokken ni? Klokken ti?" he asked.

Lingo pointed at her watch.

"Klokken elleve? Lad os komme igang! Hurtigt!" They only had one hour until the party.

Hvad er klokken? = what time is it?; **Klokken ni** = nine o'clock; **Klokken ti** = ten o'clock; **Klokken elleve** = eleven o'clock; **Lad os komme igang** = let's go; **Hurtigt** = quick

Chef Peter and Lingo whizzed around the kitchen:

Et forklæde til dig.

Et piskeris.

En røreskål.

Et forklæde til dig = an apron for you; **Et piskeris** = a whisk; **En røreskål** = a mixing bowl

"Giv mig venligst smør, sukker, æg og mel," said Chef.

Lingo wasn't sure what those words meant, so she just grabbed fish, coffee and onions instead.

"Fisk, kaffe og løg. Ulækkert!" laughed Chef.

Giv mig venligst = please give me; **smør** = butter; **sukker** = the sugar; **æg** = egg; **mel** = flour; **og** = and; **fisk** = fish; **kaffe** = coffee; **løg** = onions; **Ulækkert** = diisgusting

Chef plopped sugar, butter, eggs and flour into a bowl. "So that's what 'smør, sukker, æg og mel' means!" laughed Lingo.

"Jeg blander, du blander, vi blander," said Chef and together they began to mix the cake.

Jeg blander = I mix; **du blander** = you mix; **vi blander** = we mix

"Til sidst bagepulver. To skefulde," said Chef. Lingo guessed 'bagepulver' meant baking powder, but how much?

Before she could ask, Chef hurried away, saying, "Undskyld mig, jeg er nødt til at tisse."

Lingo laughed, "I can guess what 'tisse' means!"

Til sidst = finally; **bagepulver** = baking powder; **To skefulde** = two spoonfulls; **Undskyld mig** = excuse me; **jeg er nødt til at tisse** = I need to do a wee wee

I wonder if this is too much? thought Lingo as she added ten spoonfulls of 'bagepulver' to the mix.

She carefully put everything into the oven and before long, a sweet cakey smell filled the kitchen.

powdr pobi = baking powder

"Hvad skete der? Den er kæmpestor!" said Chef.

Lingo realised she had added too much baking powder.
"Sorry," she said sheepishly.

Hvad skete der? = what happened; **Den er kæmpestor** = it's huge

"I know what will make you feel better," said Lingo, kindly. "Eat this 'pickle'!"

"Ulækkert. Jeg hader pickles," said Chef.

They were running out of time.

Ulækkert = disgusting; **Jeg hader pickles** = I hate gherkins

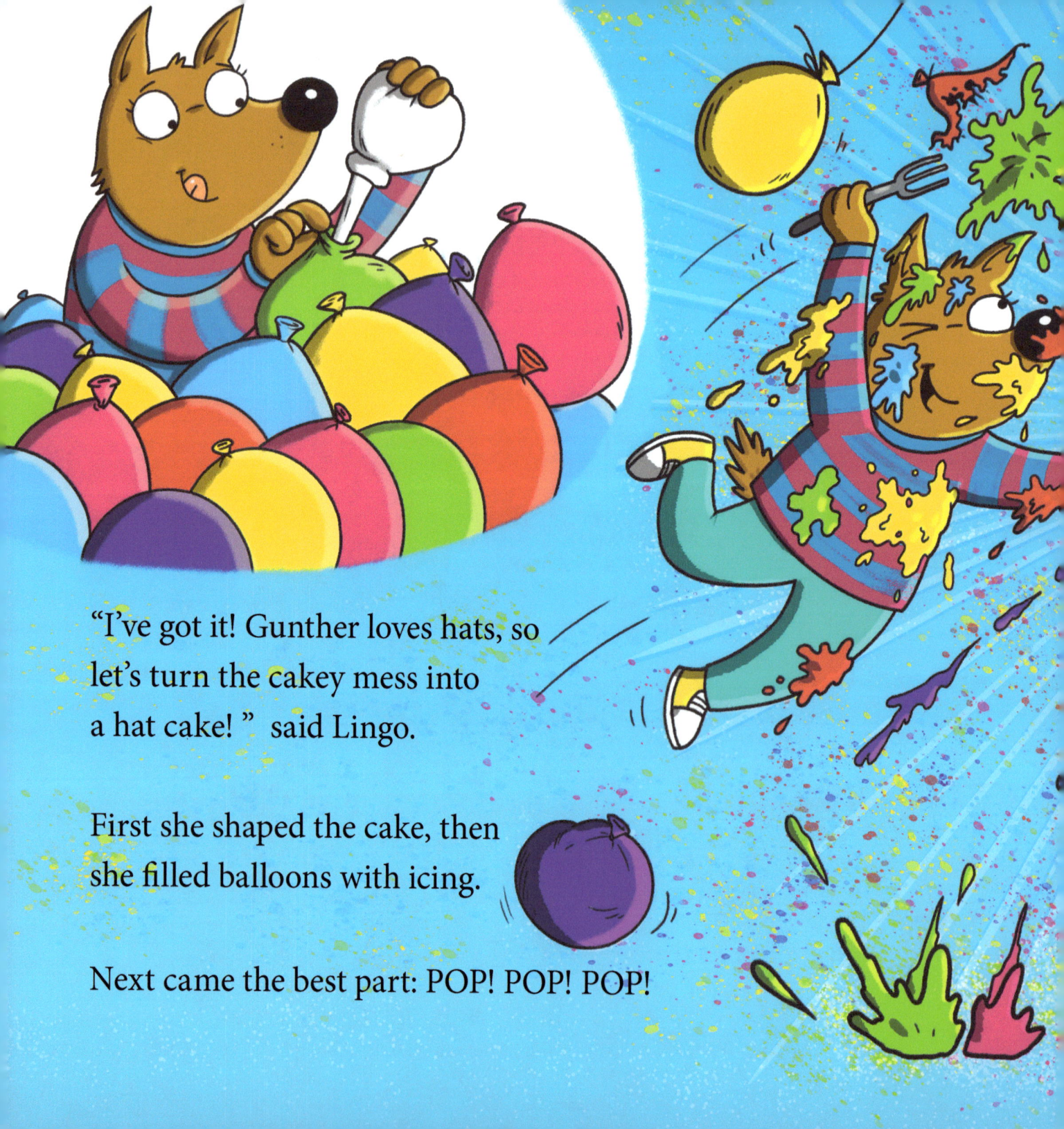

"I've got it! Gunther loves hats, so let's turn the cakey mess into a hat cake!" said Lingo.

First she shaped the cake, then she filled balloons with icing.

Next came the best part: POP! POP! POP!

It was a messy job but in the end, the cake looked fantastic.
"Rød, orange, gul, grøn, blå. Fantastisk!" said Chef.

Rød = red; **orange** = orange; **gul** = yellow; **grøn** = green; **blå** = blue; **Fantastisk** = fantastic

There was a knock at the door.
"Døren!" said Chef.
It was Gunther, and he was wearing his special hat!

"Thankyou. This makes me feel so special," said Gunther.
"You are special," replied Lingo.

Døren = the door

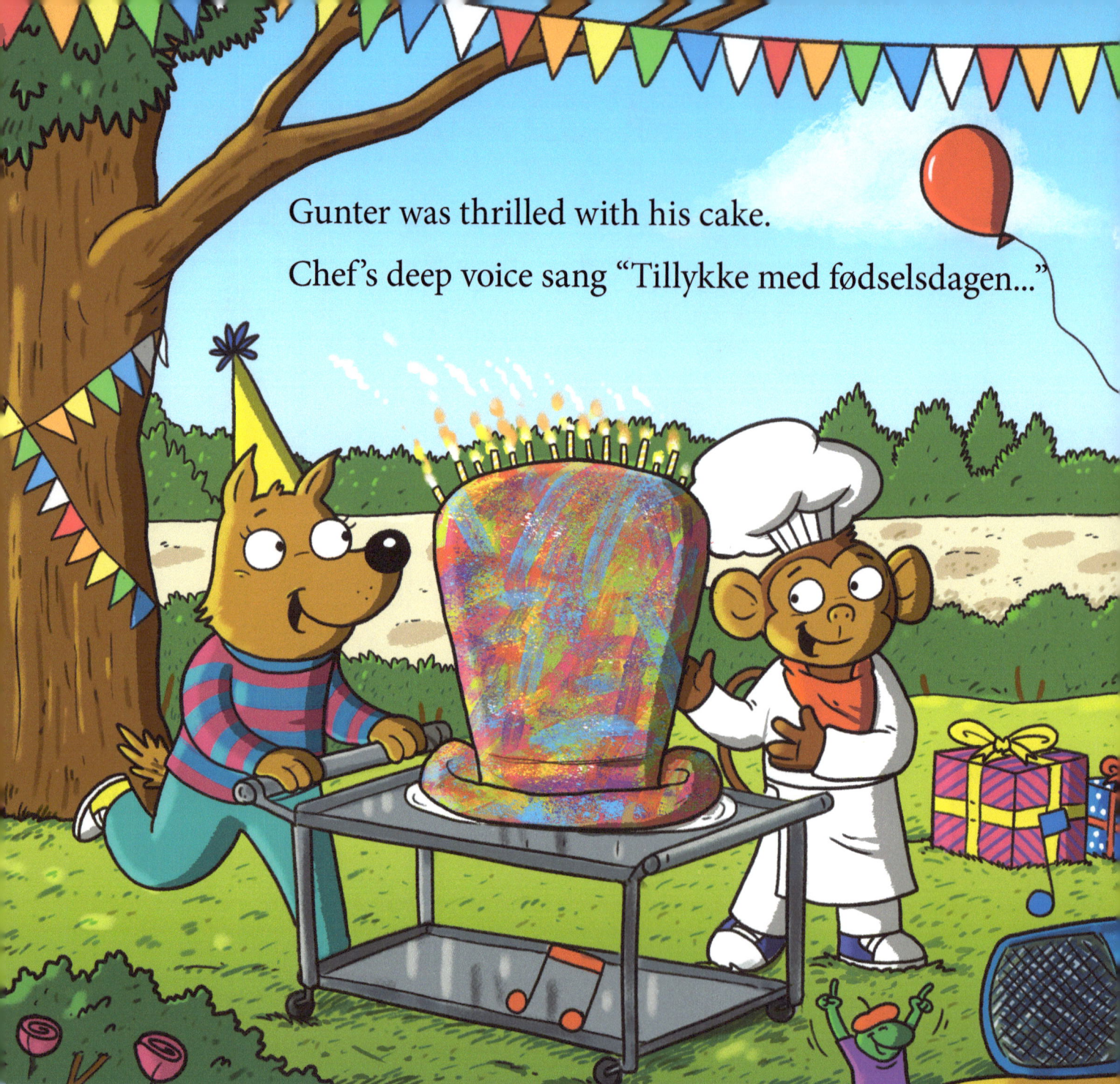

Gunter was thrilled with his cake.

Chef's deep voice sang "Tillykke med fødselsdagen..."

Tillykke med fødselsdagen = happy birthday to you

"Pust!" said Chef.

Gunther blew out all the candles in one puff and everyone tucked in.

pust = blow

"Jeg spiser, du spiser, han spiser, hun spiser, de spiser," laughed Chef.

"Vi spiser," added Lingo proudly.

Jeg spiser = I eat; **du spiser** = you eat; **han spiser** = he eats; **hun spiser** = she eats; **de spiser** = they eat; **vi spiser** = we eat

Lingo, Gunther and Chef watched the sun go down.

"Jeg er glad,
du er glad,
vi er alle glade," said Chef.

Jeg er glad = I am happy; **du er glad** = you are happy; **Vi er alle glade** = we are all happy

Baking a cake, helping a friend, learning a new language... what a day!

But now it was time for bed. It was time to dream about all the fun things that might happen tomorrow.

Learning to love languages

An additional language opens a child's mind, broadens their horizons and enriches their emotional life. Research has shown that the time between a child's birth and their sixth or seventh birthday is a "golden period" when they are most receptive to new languages. This is because they have an in-built ability to distinguish the sounds they hear and make sense of them. The Story-powered Language Learning Method taps into these natural abilities.

How the Story-powered language learning Method works

We create an emotionally engaging and funny story for children and adults to enjoy together, just like any other picture book. Studies show that social interaction, like enjoying a book together, is critical in language learning.

Through the story, we introduce a relatable character who speaks only in the new language. This helps build empathy and a positive attitude towards people who speak different languages. These are both important aspects in laying the foundations for lasting language acquisition in a child's life.

As the story progresses, the child naturally works with the characters to discover the meanings of a wide range of fun new words. Strategic use of humour ensures that this subconscious learning is rewarded with laughter; the child feels good and the first seeds of a lifelong love of languages are sown.

For more information and free learning resources visit www.neuwestendpress.com

You can learn more words and phrases with these hilarious, heartwarming stories from NEU WESTEND PRESS

Available in over 50 different languages!

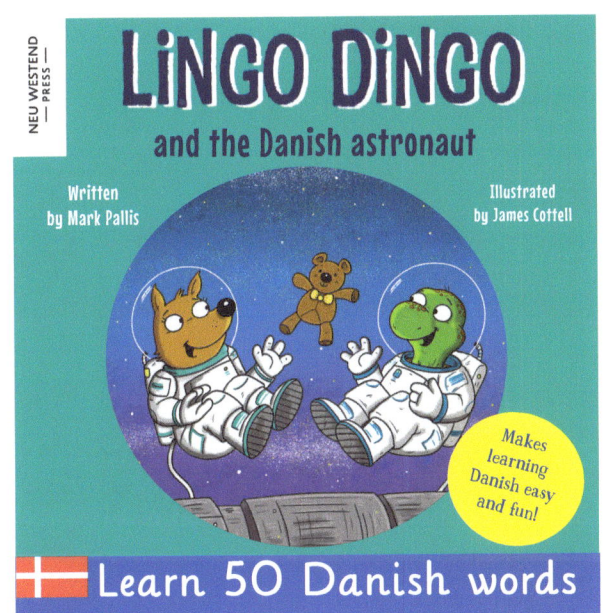

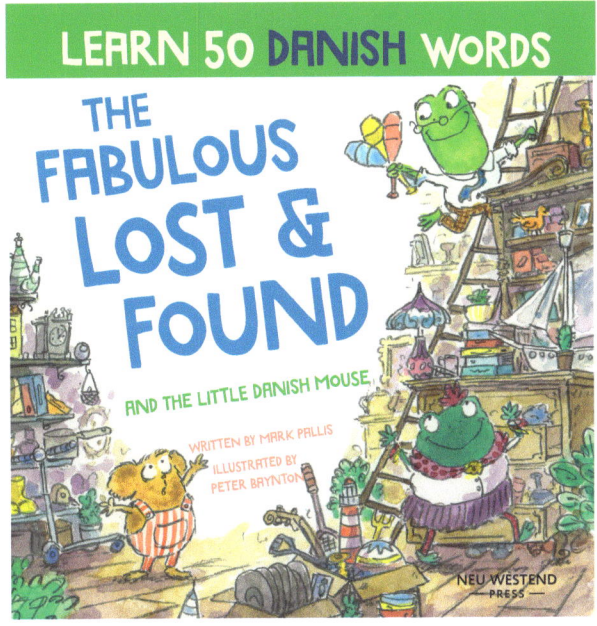

@MARK_PALLIS on twitter
www.markpallis.com

To download your FREE certificate, and more cool stuff, visit
www.neuwestendpress.com

@jamescottell on INSTAGRAM
www.jamescottellstudios.co.uk

"I want people to be so busy laughing, they don't realise they're learning!"
Mark Pallis

Crab and Whale is the bestselling story of how a little Crab helps a big Whale. It's carefully designed to help even the most energetic children find a moment of calm and focus. It also includes a special mindful breathing exercise and affirmation for children. Also available in French, Spanish and German.

Featured as one of Mindful.org's 'Seven Mindful Children's books'

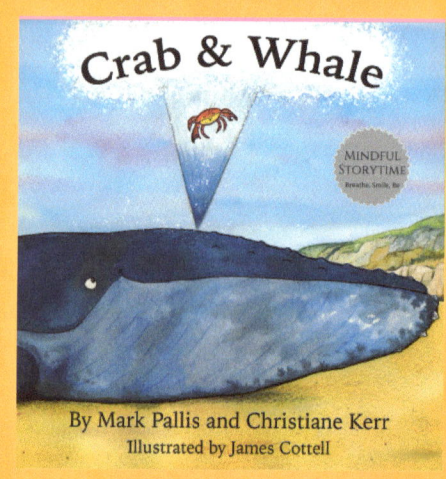

Do you call them hugs or cuddles?

In this funny, heartwarming story, you will laugh out loud as two loveable gibbons try to figure out if a hug is better than a cuddle and, in the process, learn how to get along.

A perfect story for anyone who loves a hug (or a cuddle!)

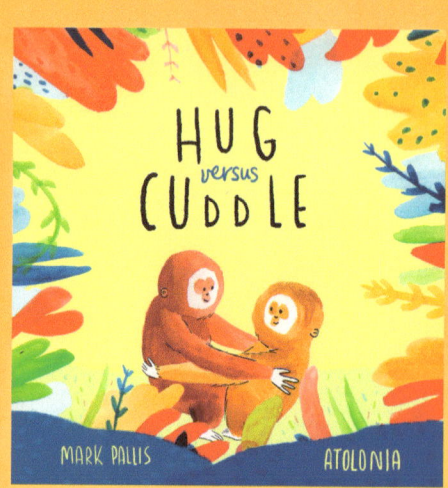

www.markpallis.com

www.ingramcontent.com/pod-product-compliance
Lightning Source LLC
Chambersburg PA
CBHW040021130526
44590CB00036B/43